land of dream and dreamer

poems of Ireland

Maureen Grady

For my Rose, with
all the love
of my
heart.

Bambaz Press

Los Angeles 2019

Book Layout: Baz Here and Maureen Grady
Cover Photo: Maureen Grady
Author photo: John Botte

Bambaz Press
548 S. Spring Street Suite 1201
Los Angeles, CA 90013
bambi@bambazpress.com

ISBN: 9781701576353

for my parents
Roberta Faith Patterson Grady
& Stafford Robert Grady,
magnificent Irish souls,
and for all the dreamers before and after

We are the music makers, and we are the dreamers of dreams.

O'Shaughnessy

I

Long Last Look

The women who left
stood at the railing of emigrant ships
watching those who loved them
wave handkerchiefs in the air.

And further along the coast
the women who stayed
pulled white sheets
from their beds,
from their clotheslines,
and ran out to the western cliff edge
to bid goodbye
as the big ships headed
into rough Atlantic waters.

The women who stayed
cried out, voices hoarse in great gales,
waving their large linen flags of farewell.

And they never forgot
the faces of those who left.

On the deck,
the sea-bound passengers
sailed toward a new life,
heavy with grief and hope.
Breathing in the whole of home
with a long last look
they seared into memory.

Few ever returned.

To their dying days those who left
held fast to that final farewell:

the last look,
the cries of women,
the white sheets,
wingèd on the wind.

II

Sheath

Let's go back to the first divisions
between stars and space,
darkness and light,
water and earth.

All borne out of the glance of God.

And into the vast immensity
of the Atlantic Ocean
descended a small kingdom
called by many names
Ériu, Iveriu, Juverna,
Hibernia - land of winter,
Éire, Ireland.

This prayer of landscape
was a sheath of beauty
against the cruelty of the world.

Herself

As her mind faded,
she saw the beloved horses of her youth
flying through the trees outside her home.
Daily she went out to the woods in search of buried treasure,
poking the earth with a sword, carrying a serpent-headed staff.

She'd eat little, but relished her almond cake and tea.
Then at dusk, she waited for the crow who watched her
from the hazel branch outside the kitchen window.
When night fell, she folded into herself.

She remembered her renowned beauty of days past,
her long auburn hair now silver,
but she'd forgotten the names of men who had loved her,
and those of the men she'd loved.

Though her gloves, keys and glasses eluded her,
and present time slipped into a soft roundness,
she could still see her girlhood in Galway, as clear as day.

An Auspicious Star

Crossing from Galway
into Mayo,
Leenane to Delphi,
we drove in sacred silence
along the rugged coast.

At the mouth of the valley,
a shooting star,
against the vast sea of sky,
blazed
as sudden as love.

Ahhhhhh

Golden.
Glorious.
Gone.

Famine: Black '47

In the winter of that year
the Queen's landlords feasted as always.
And when they ventured out to inspect
their post-eviction properties,
they saw the blighted, black potato fields,
the dying and the dead.
They held fine French silk scarves
up to their faces to mask the stench.

Next to the road
in a ditch the dying lay,
raving with fever and puking yellow bile.
By the hawthorn tree
a woman, long dead,
her stomach distended,
pregnant with starvation.

Not far from her, two lovers,
their frozen bodies under a single shawl,
their mouths, teeth, tongues stained green from grass,
the last thing left on earth to eat.

By summer,
only their bones were visible
in the fragrant bog,
stark and chalk-white,
pounded by rains,
howling in the wind,
gleaming in the thistle.

Sea Bed

Let us go there,
plumb the mysteries,
seek the wonders,
in that deepest
blue.

O vast world,
teeming with life!
We'll find depths
never reached before.

I dive down deep,
holding my breath
until that day.

Ériu

The ancient land of Ireland
called Ériu, daughter of Dé Dannan,
was the body of the goddess.

And the green isle,
the mystic kingdom,
sang of her shape,
her curves - fields, hills,
mountains, valleys.

The sea surrounded her,
and the wild winds tossed
the tendrils of her hair.

She was of a strength never before seen,
a body born to endure the yoke,
the heartbreak of colony, religion, shame,
famine, silence, war, exile.

Despite immense sorrow,
incalculable loss,
the imaginings of a great culture rose up in her.
Songs, poems, music, legends.

These golden gifts lived on
in those who inhabited the body,
and their descendants,
ever after.

Redemption

There's a lonesome air
in the west of Ireland
where a young girl jumped
from the high cliffs,
binding herself to death,
to the famished rock,
to a shroud of sea.

And falling there,
the fierce wind,
unrelenting,
lifted her up again,
bound her feet to land,
to life,
howling
not yet,
not here,
not in this way;
it is not your time.

Umami

taste of the earth
mushroom
spud
cabbage
root

taste is pure mystery

the shock of it
sweet sour
bitter bold
sharp soft
spicy mild

taste of salt water
origin of life
oyster mussel
hake salmon

the palate changes
as do we
the palate evolves
as must we

we are taken
by nature's alchemy
somewhere new

burrowing our way
back to the earth

swimming our way
back to the sea

Glass Heart

I dreamt I loved a glass blower
and that he loved me too.
He blew me a glass heart
of swirling molten purple
forged from fire, powder,
and the breath of his life,
and told me it would never break.

Then I woke.

Fields of Memory

Even on the last day of his life,
an old Irish man in the Bronx
could repeat the names of every field
from his childhood,
fields he had not seen in decades,
fields he would never see again.

He had carried his native landscape
with him always,
counting internally,
naming infernally,
each field,
in perfect order
all the way to the sea.

Looking out on the tenements,
he conjured green before his eyes,
whispered his dearest ones:
the field of the stone of the cats,
the field of the farmer's curse,
the field of the holy well.

On the Death of Seamus Heaney

The wordsmith breathes
and fashions letters into gold,
carves thoughts out of air,
molds perfect form,
shifts our consciousness,
conjures what could not be dreamed of.

And with two faint words of final wisdom,
Nolle timiri, he left us.
Do not be afraid, he consoled,
facing death with that last offering.
He went alone to the island he'd envisioned.
The digging had been done.

What words are there for loss of him,
words of what he would call *inner radiance,*
words that only he could summon?

Siren Song

How long have you been out on the ocean?

In a dark pub,
we two listen to a piece of spoken word as it casts a spell.
Something about the sea, a legend, an origin of water.

My mother was a mermaid
My father, King Neptune

As the perfomer on stage weaves a myth,
his hand closes around my waist,
draws me in, as do the lyrics,
the tune, his closeness, his intent.

I was born on the crest of a wave
And I was rocked in the cradle of the deep

Our hands interwine.
The piper's whistling pierces us through.
Now for the heart's renewal.

Seaweed and barnacles are my clothes

His fingers move through my hair,
reminding me I have come from the sea.
I will not draw him down to a drowning depth,
but perhaps he will me.

Cow Circle

I sat in a field of damp grass,
in the very center
of a Neolithic stone circle,
imagining a piece of theatre
I'd love to direct there

when eight cows approached
from the far edges of the field,
came right up to me,
until their big brown heads
encircled me,
crowded above me.

And one by one,
each lay down in the softness,
their soulful eyes
asking something of me.

I breathed in
the heat of their bodies,
the clouds of warm breath,
the sweet smell of grass,
munched in perfect rhythm.

And then,
a pure peace pervaded,
one that came from
ancient animal wisdom,
and field, stone circle, and sky.

Holy Trinity

A pilgrim
travels differently,
carries an inner landscape,
ponders meaning.

A mystic
sees the reality of the invisible
and coexists there,
within the visible world.

An artist
lives twice,
in both time and in art,
seeking to make tangible,
and hoping to make immortal,
what it means to be alive.

Nollaig na mBan: *Little Christmas*

Irish women gather by the fire
on the Feast of the Epiphany,
a day reserved for them alone,
the only of the year.

Fathers,
sons,
uncles,
brothers,
go out to
the fields,
the factories,
the boats,
the pubs,
and give the women
their *little Christmas*,

And on this solitary day,
away from
cleaning,
cooking,
knitting,
sewing,
woman's work that's never done,
they revel in the company of each other:
mothers,
daughters,
aunts,
sisters.

In the warmth of the room,
the heat of womens' bodies
peat smoke and coal,
candle wax dripping,
they hold fast to this sacred time and space:

laughter,
love,
loss,
worry,
stories,
gossip,
compliments -
pouring the tea,
pouring the milk,
pouring the whiskey,
pouring their hearts out.

Safe Home

Just before parting
the poet said something in Irish
about truth and the eyes of a cat.
But I could not hold it;
I could not remember.

Only felt the round weight of it,
the still, disguised arrow,
the stone upon which to build a new life.

"Safe home," the poet said.
The air brightened around us.
Take me with you, I did not say.
Home. Ireland. You.

To the Boy Who Died on Clare Island

I wanted to cross over to the island
to honor you, as local friends had done.
You whom I never knew.

One learns to drive early on an island.
Perhaps too early, it seems.
An old car, a narrow road, a fatal ditch.

You died instantly, the Mayo paper said.

After midnight it was,
the morning never greeted you.

When I was just your age, just thirteen,
I loved a boy who died like you
though an icy road was for him the hand of death.

Your mother and I share a name.
And though I will never know her,
I grieve for her. I hold her in my heart.

I hold my own son closer still.

The Price

At the Abbey Theatre,
the holiday matinee of *Kathleen ni Houlihan*
by Yeats and Lady Gregory was canceled
as word of rebellion spread,
just blocks away at the General Post Office.

This was to be the day.
April 24, 1916, Easter Monday.

Sean Connolly, lead actor, took his cue,
and after playing the part of a rebel for years,
he grabbed a rifle from the stash hidden under the stage,
and ran for O'Connell Street to become one.

He was the first rebel to die that day.

Nellie Bushell, the usher on call,
and Barney Murphy, the stage hand, followed suit.
They armed themselves and poured out into the Dublin day,
joining the patriots- poets, playwrights, teachers, revolutionaries.
All were prepared to give their lives.

Back at the theatre,
the now dark stage
gave off a ghostly glow.
The play that did not play
hung in the ether.

Kathleen ni Houlihan,
the old woman who embodied Ireland,
had four green fields worth dying for:
Connaught, Munster, Leinster, Ulster.
That day she was both myth and prophet.
She foresaw a generation of young men
dying for Ireland.

The play
that did not play that day
foretold
that the *red-cheeked would be pale,*
the *good broken,*
and the *children of Ireland*
would be without fathers
at their christenings.

This was to be the price
to birth a country.

One hundred years later
to the day,
as I heard the Proclamation read again
in front of the GPO,
I wanted to kneel down,
while children dressed as dead patriots
chased each other down O'Connell Street.

Pulling In

Darkness descends,
and winter
far before its time
in the west.

Night falls fast,
and day after day,
wind and rain
ensure that
the evenings are
pulling in,
as the people are,
pulling inward,
into their homes,
into their hearth fires,
into themselves.

The Piper is Pan
for Brendan Keegan

Flute, reed, whistle, pipe.
His fingers move
fast as hummingbirds,
his feet pound the earth
drawing forth fire from the Source.

Here stands a rustic god,
sparks of mischief in the eyes,
at one with fields and groves,
shepherds, nymphs and wooded glens.

His instrument is his own
life force breathing through him,
and the ancient sylvan sounds hold us captive
with something unremembered
within our own bodies, our own breath.

The night is awash with stars,
and rain and winds lash the low-lying islands of Clew Bay.

And though we are far in time and place
from the heat and sun and sands of Greece,
and the early nature gods,
I am sure he must be, like Pan,
the only piper to open the gate of dawn.

Another Life

I recognize the hand
moving across my face,
a poet's.

So many years ago,
a man, in a fierce country,
loved a woman.

I remember the insistent pull,
the shy sea-eyes,
my hair woven with leaves.

They lived a life.

I recall his voice,
a purr, a hum in the darkness,
the grave face.

There. Then.

I remember the fingers
seeking something
as if blind.

It was long ago.

Where have you been, he asks.

Here.

Now.

Always.

Revolutionary Ducks, Easter 1916

St Stephen's Green
at the city's heart
promised one square block of peace
in midst of the Easter Rising.

There,
James Kearney, park greenskeeper,
fulfilled his daily devotion
to Dublin's waterfowl
despite the rebellion
sweeping Dublin.

The Irish Citizens Army demanded
of the British forces opposing them,
a single sacred daily hour
of ceasefire to feed the ducks.

Gunfire was silenced.
The ducks were fed.
And war began again.

A Leenane Session

Dark and bright this room,
and pulsing with the blood of instruments.
Furtive sideways glances and downcast eyes
of the men from the glan who never married,
wearing their solitude and their histories
like woolen winter coats.

An old man in the far corner
sings of a longing for love that is palpable;
it hangs in the air, flowering among us.

By the window, a rugged man
begins to sing of heroic times with a force that is true.
The others join the chorus, a low warm hum.

The sunburned farmer next to me
leans in, asks would I give up a poem.
How does he know I write them?
I would give all to this land, to these my people,
but this night I want to take all in.

As the music shifts,
a young girl begins to step dance in the midst of us,
her arms rigid as a bound people,
but her feet vital, triumphant,
asking something of the earth.

But my heart is drawn to the one who leads the others.
He sings of lost love in Venezuela
with all himself, all his goodness.
His humble smile flashes brightly at the close
as a cheer goes up.

Then he offers his young cousin next to him
the safe space to sing a song of death,
infuses him with strength.

His hands move deftly
from one instrument to another,
yet later when we speak,
he denies even being a musician,
deflects all praise to the others.
Then, to reach him,
I tell him something I know of him
he recognizes as true,
and a golden thread binds us
for a moment.

He had climbed the holy mountain at dawn that day,
and he seemed to carry it within him
as he disappeared into the ink black night.

Turf as Offering

In autumn,
parting from the western isles,
turf fires would be left
burning in the hearth,
a gift of sorts from islanders,
a hope, a silent prayer
that their cottage homes,
would withstand the harsh winter
yet to come.

The summer before
the turf was cut, sliced, stacked, dried,
then packed high in the shed,
the two last pieces of sod
forming a cross.

Earth, root, leaf, grass,
plant, manure, moss.
The bog claims the men of this land,
carries the ancestral memory of a people.

Earth as talisman,
earth as offering.
From this we come forth,
to this we return.

Irish Grammar

In Irish,
we say that a feeling
is with, at, or upon us.
Sorrow is with me.
Anger is at me.
Love is upon me.

We do not have a feeling;
it has us.

we are not the feeling
The feeling is with us

I am sad
I am depressed
I am happy

A Warning from Aristotle

The gods may take human form,
warned Aristotle.

The way, as we were talking,
he slid his wedding band
thick and shining
from his left ring finger
and twirled it round
between his right thumb and forefinger,
gave me pause.

The sun shone on us that day,
in a land of constant rain.
Beans on toast and tea with milk we ate,
peasant food made noble.

And after,
orange cake with chocolate icing,
sweet as his smile.

As he walked away,
not to be seen again,
the grey Dublin street shimmered silver.

The Wide Net

It is an ancient and green land.
It is raining.
It is fierce.
Those who see the unseen are heeded.

I know things.
My voice carries to the far hills.
The people are hungry,
no words can fill them.
They chant hymns of woe, of war, of loss.

I have the gift of sight.
I look into the sea, the mother of us.
I watch the curraghs go out at break of day.
I know where the fish are.
I see where the fishermen must throw their nets.

I watch these men,
heavy with life, with rain, go forth.
I see the gold and silver fish, the life underwater.
Their nets are flung, woven from my hair,
yet in the dream they hold.

Then the nets rise, plentiful.
The fish feed my people, more than mere grass has done.
Sweet sounds of life are heard again.
Sad songs are remembered.

Sean Nós

There are those who sing sad Irish love songs.
And there are those who live them, and may not sing.

Throwing My Wedding Band into Irish Waters

At the moment the boat moved past the Delphi Valley,
where echoes of the famine cry out along the granite shore,
I heard my soul-self speak, *here, now,*
and slipped my wedding band from my finger.

I turned it once to read the initials, and the date,
then dropped the sacred golden ring,
symbol of the beloved, the eternal,
into Irish waters.

I have chosen this place,
the aperture of that valley,
the stone inlet, a molten emerald vale,
where they say more starved in 1847
than in any other place of pain.

The ring bobbed, at first,
the sea rough with wave and foam,
a flash, a gleam, current-carried,
then sank into oblivion.

There, at the moment of parting,
with rain cooling the searing pain of it,
water, wind, rock, and sky
were the only truths I knew.

This is a land where belief is all.
God. Nation. Church. Vow.
I had believed also.
My finger wore the imprint of half a lifetime,
a pale flesh ring where no sun had been.

Sometimes in my dreams,
I dive to find my wedding band.
I comb the silt, the sludge,
digging, clawing,
frantic to find it, lungs straining.

At last I see a glint of gold
in the murky depths,
half-sunken in sand.
Despite the longing, despite the loss,
I do not pick it up again,
but rise to the sea's surface,
to the dappled light.
I rise to the living air.

A Man is an Island

He is an island
I visit in my mind,
island of otherness,
island of mystery.

There breathes a holy happiness,
we carve it out of stone.
He is the keeper of the flame;
I write the poems to live in.

We are both young and old there,
and time is not apace,
just the vast sea to enclose us,
night stars to crowd us with their fires.

He is an island
I visit in my heart,
island of oneness,
island of clarity.

And from that fair isle of rock and green,
one pure place of peace,
we hurt no living thing.

Angels of Tea
for Jo Flinn

As long as the tea is piping hot,
the brown bread warm,
the butter rich,
Irish mothers can carry the world
upon their shoulders,
greet any day or person,
withstand anything,
withstand everything,
Birth, death, loss,
constant rain,
each crying child.

They are angels of tea
gathering, nourishing,
nurturing, mending,
pouring out the warmth,
bracing with their strength.

The fields outside are lush,
the cows milked, the hens laying.
Entering the kitchen,
if the kettle is on,
the bread rising,
and the table laid,
all's right with world.

This is the daily holy communion
of the Irish mother.
Brown bread and tea, not wine,
and the rich Irish butter,
not present at the Last Supper.

Forgetting a Few Words of Yeats

It had never happened before.
I knew it as my own name:
The Song of Wandering Aengus.
My very favorite poem.

But the shock of him knowing it,
loving it too,
wanting to share it,
needing to share it,
that's what made me falter
on two of the words
I knew by heart,
just as he twice faltered.

But together aloud
in the night air,
on the Westport street,
word after word,
line by line,
we found it,
we knew it,
and we both finally had it,
had it by heart.

The Breathing Burren

There is a world apart,
of elemental beauty carved by glacier,
where tiny wildflowers
pierce through limestone.

No trees grace this rare realm,
a silver stone land with
not enough water to drown,
nor earth to bury,
but fauna and flora
half-hidden, abundant.

Only here
on the vast crust of Earth
do flowers from the Arctic,
the Mediterranean,
and the high Alps
grow side by side
and flourish.

And briefly, in spring,
out of the grey limestone,
the early purple orchid breaks through,
the crowning glory,
the one that draws forth love.

Outer Beauty

Would that my love
become my outer beauty,
become a form irresistible,
make it as impossible
not to love me,
as it's impossible
to unlove him.

Too Many Trees

The farmer who lived alone
on the hill above the lough
had not enough light to live by.

And when he took his life
one midwinter day
too many trees was whispered
by the locals to be the cause of death.

Darkness descended early upon that land.

The Sting, The Honey

The moment shocks,
sharp – stab – sting,
an arrow in the chest.

Everything changes.

Flushed across the left breast,
the perfect pain grows every hour,
quickens, swells over the heart.

The fire of it spreads,
the body heats,
the world spins.

Nothing will ever be the same.

The bee is mighty,
the sting pointed,
but Cupid's arrow more so.

There is the pain, yes,
but then there is the honey,
the golden honey,
love.

The Harp Speaks

Ancient Irish harps were made from the felled trees
of the land - ash, sycamore, beech, cherry,
oak, yew, poplar, walnut and elm.

And the music of each harp sang of the specific wood.
Gut strings from the bodies of animals were plucked by deft
fingers,
blood and heat had coursed through them, had primal power.

Beloved by kings, each court would boast a harpist
of high renown, playing their poems and psalms,
shedding sweetness on the air.

But as Ireland rose up, searching for herself,
the harp sang out resistance to the Crown.
It was forbidden, all harps were burned,
tossed in tall pyres where sound became smoke.

Now they live again.
Formed like an ancient hunter's bow,
each harp is in pursuit of something.
And the music is an arrow of pure beauty
shot out into the world.

Messenger

There is something religious about a hawk in a high tree.
The ancient Celts knew them to be messengers
between this world and the next.
Wingèd, fierce, they can fall as fireballs,
able to cross between spheres
as humans cannot.

When my parents died,
there seemed no earthly way to escape the grief,
the natural world offered little solace.
I longed only to touch that other world,
touch them again,
shed the unbearable weight,
leave my lost body,
fly.

Then—a sudden gift.
In a primeval Irish wood,
I held fast to the gaze of a hawk.
It seemed to say
you can visit the dead.

I learned I could step away
from this life,
lift myself up,
travel heavenward,
hover between two worlds at once.

I had loved that Merlin himself was a falconer,
gave Arthur a magical education—
to transform himself into birds and animals,
to metabolize wisdom, embody bravery,
to be a good king,
to be a noble king.

Moving between this world and the next,
with wings of spirit,
I understood there is a realm most true
where my parents, and I,
Merlin, Arthur, and the hawk,
are all one.

Heavenly Phenomena

I went out to meet,
in one blessed night,
three heavenly phenomena
as promised in the morning paper:
the lunar eclipse,
the snow moon,
a blazing comet,

but storm clouds
obscured them all.

So I closed my eyes,
still seeking to see,
and listened to the silence,
sensing what was there
behind the clouds,
behind it all,
behind all.

Chasing a Poem

What passes you, is not for you, so say the Irish.

Sometimes I hear a poem
rise up from the land.
Or sometimes it comes toward me on the wind,
a clarion diamond like the eye of . . .
something,
and then I hold my breath.

If by chance I capture it,
the seed of it, its essence,
put the poem to paper
before it fades into brightening air,
I can breathe again.

And sometimes I hear it whole,
take it into my body,
and let it tremble there for a time,
until words form
and something
new is made.

And other times I cannot grasp it;
the poem will just pass me,
glimmering,
flee back into the ether.

Perhaps the poem will find another poet.

III

American Wake for Elizabeth Howick

On a steel grey evening,
the rain in waves against her,
my grandmother locked the door
of the Kerry schoolhouse
where she taught the farmers' children
and made her way to the sea.

Stories of an unrequited love,
someone named O'Connor she had lived for,
came down through family whispers.
She was only a girl of eighteen,
leaving the schoolhouse,
her parents, four sisters,
and all she knew.

She crossed the country on foot.
Rock, thistle, rain.
Eight days later she reached Queenstown
and boarded the *Campania* for New York.
It was the first day of spring.

I imagine her on the deck,
windswept, gaunt,
her eyes holding the last light
of green land
she would never see again,
her mind full of poems she knew by heart,
words shaped by stone, hills, faith, famine.

Ten days later at Ellis Island
she signed the manifest,
Lizzie Howick,
a new self for a new world,
and stepped into the April morning.

No word of her ever reached home.

She died too young,
widowed, penniless,
leaving two strong girls to grace the earth.

In the faded picture that remains,
her dark hair pulled back,
the eyes deep-set,
her thick brows,
the sharp cheekbones,
her lips a fierce straight line,
I see my mother and myself.
I see my daughter.

Deep thanks for belief, encouragement, generosity, and inspiration

Jack & Lori Grapes
John & Joan L'Heureux
Peggy & Russell Tunder
Elicia Ho
John Botte
Carina & Ciela Courtright
Gabrielle Kelly
Maire Moriarty
Vinny Browne
Brendan Keegan
John Hegarty
Joanne Keegan
Catherine O'Grady
Michael Moran
Clodagh Bower
Maureen O'Grady Ford
Julia Curran
Srinath & Renu Samudrala
Bronwyn Reed
Aidan Reed
Stafford & Peg Grady
Shaun & Audrey Grady
Kevin & Kim Raftery
Tom Reed
Adam Croasdale
Rachel Rath & Kevin Marron
Ray Barry & Robyn Mundell
Jane Olson
Caroline & Noor Youness
Jean & Peter Vaughn
Bryan Delaney
Catherine Eaton
Sonya Macari & Colin Devlin
Frank Benson
Scan O'Connor
Mark Foyle
Michael Wade
Danny Sheehy
Ailbhe Barrett
Margaret & Jackie Joyce
Marty Joyce
Carl Faichne
Barry Flinn
Jo & Hugo Flinn

Kate Crowley
Finn Wittrock
Lisa Krueger
Sally Krueger-Wyman
Fiona O'Brien
Bryana Tunder
Vittoria Colonna
Amar Singh
Eleni Lambros
Helen Lambros
Fotini Dimou
Monsignor Connolly
Fionnula Flanagan
Jason Patric
Anne Fleming
Valeria Golino
Niall McKay
Marissa Aroy
Tim Ruddy
Bebe Nyiri
Daniel Nyiri
Claire Harrison
Johanna O'Connor
Tom & Imelda O'Connor
Patricia O'Brien
Tess O'Brien
Rupert Knox
Michael Sutherland
Zsu Zsa Holp
Eszter Knipl
Madi Holdsworth
Catherine Siggins
Veronica Houlihan
Jim McInerny
Kate McInerny
Brendan Grady
Donal & Eileen Moriarty
Deborah Kolar
Ernesto D'Argenio
Mauro Di Silvestre
Riccardo Abate
The Flinn Family
Sally Specht & Michael Trim
Paddy & Julia Foyle

Mary & Sean Hegarty
Ann Marie Lee
Katy McCollum
Kelan Barry Thomas
Molly Taylor
Robyn Guibert
Diana Van de Kamp
Julia & Paddy Foyle
Kevin McCann
Dubrays, Dublin
The Marlton, NYC
Tigh Áine, Dunquin
Bewleys, Dublin
Cake Café, Dublin
Dingle Bookshop
Cupan Tae, Galway
Charlie Byrnes Bookshop
Avoca Café, Wicklow
Tigh Neachtain, Galway
John O'Donoghue
James Ragan
Tera Vale Ragan
Vanessa Romero
Dori Koll
Isabella Kestermann
Paula Walker
Erin Dignam
Mena Kalokoh
Aminata Kalokoh
Victoria Hauzy
Megan McCaslin
Aisling Bower
Sam Sax
Jenn McGuirk
Hannah Crowley
CIACLA
Druids Hall
Amy Jelliffe
Pam Griffiths
Kate Dowd
RADISHA
Bambaz Press
Daniel Cooper

Maureen Grady is both an Irish and American citizen. She is a writer, actor, producer and teacher. She has taught British and Irish Literature, Shakespeare, and Creative Writing for many years. Her private creative writing conservatory has nurtured many young women writers. Maureen is deeply fortunate to have studied with John L'Heureux, Seamus Heaney, and Jack Grapes, and attended Eavan Boland's "Poetry and Poetics" seminar. She has won two teaching prizes: the student-nominated *One of LA's Most Inspiring Teachers,* and a national recognition for teaching creative writing from Scholastic Books given at Carnegie Hall by Tony Kushner. Maureen is a graduate of Stanford University with a BA in Literature. She also has a Masters in Theatre. She has worked in both the film industry and the theatre. Maureen is currently at work on her first play *In the Hollow* and hopes to direct her short film *Saintling* in the west of Ireland. She recently acted in the acclaimed Italian film *Euforia* which premiered at the Cannes film festival. She volunteers for the Irish Screen LA & NYC film festivals, CIACLA, for progressive political candidates and human rights causes. Maureen has two beloved grown children, and divides her time between Ireland, Italy and America.

Made in the USA
Lexington, KY
10 December 2019